To Stuart
from Kenneth
& Monay.

STARTERS
LONG AGO
BOOKS

Vikings

Macdonald Educational

Long ago there were pirates called Vikings.
They sailed in big boats
from Scandinavia.
They attacked villages and towns.

Everybody was afraid of the Vikings.
People ran to hide when they came.
The Vikings stole all their treasure
and sailed away again.

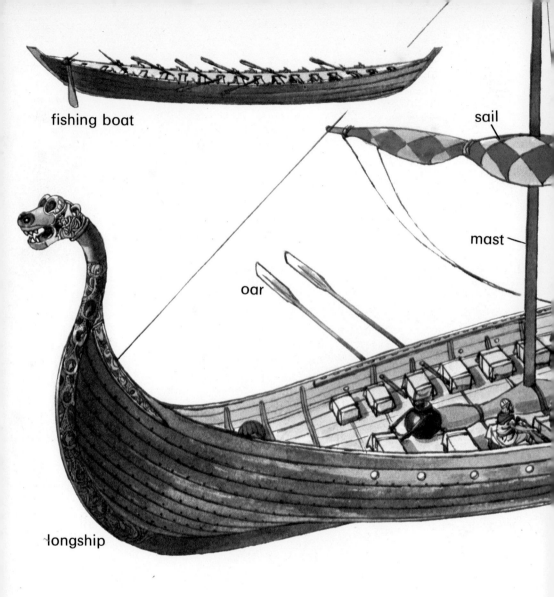

fishing boat

sail

mast

oar

longship

At home Vikings used small boats for fishing.
They used big sailing ships on long journeys
when they hunted treasure.
The big ships were called longships.

4

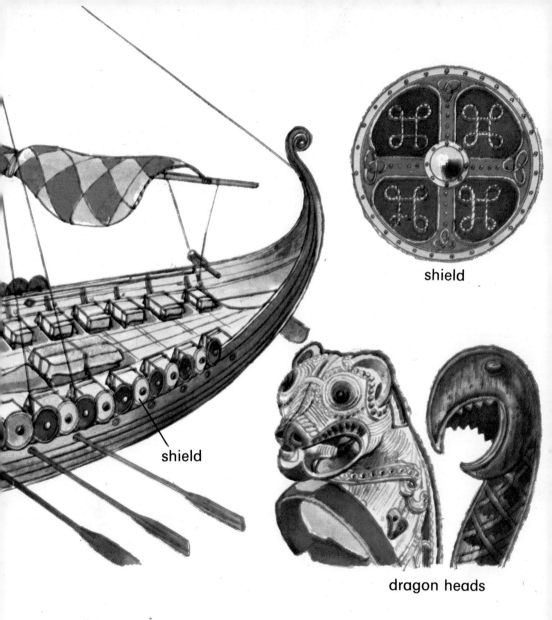

shield

shield

dragon heads

Longships had shields round the sides.
They often had a dragon head at the front.
Here are two of them.

keel

planks

Here are some Vikings building a longship.
First they made a big wooden keel.
Then they nailed planks over the keel.

6

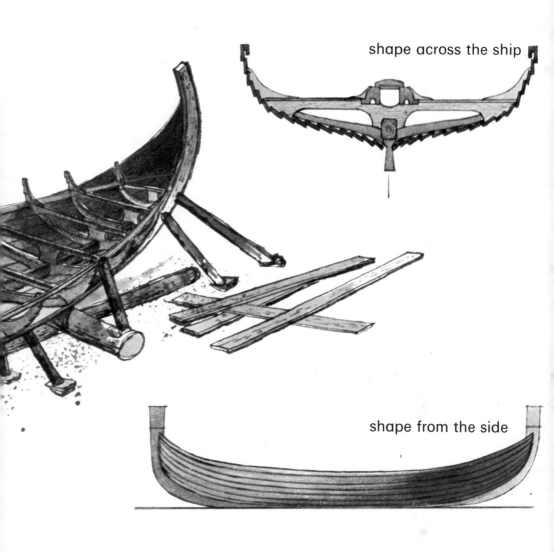

shape across the ship

shape from the side

Longships had a special shape.
This shape helped the longship to sail fast.

Churches had a lot of treasure.
The monks who looked after the church
had no weapons.
So Vikings often robbed churches.

8

Once some Vikings attacked London.
Soldiers shot arrows at them from London Bridge.
The Vikings tied ropes to the bridge.
They rowed hard and pulled the bridge down.

1. making the fire red hot

2. heating metal

4. shaping

5. sharpening the edge

Here is how a Viking sword was made.
The smith heated metal in a very hot fire.
He hammered the metal into shape.
Then he sharpened the edge.

10

3. hammering

6. attaching the handle

Viking sword

Then he put the handle on.
This handle has a beautiful pattern.
The patterns were carved in the metal.

Vikings often hunted whales.
They chased them into fiords.
Then they killed them
with swords and spears.
They used whale fat to make candles.

12

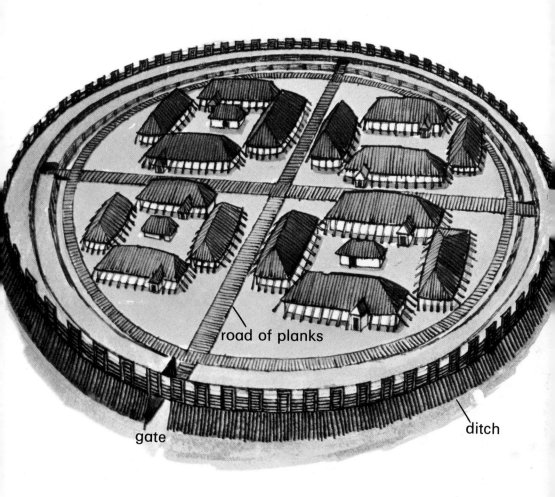

road of planks

gate

ditch

Here is a Viking camp.
For part of the year
the Vikings farmed the land.
At other times they left the camp
and went to sea as pirates.

13

Here is a house in the camp.
It is like a boat upside down.
14

chimney hole

Other Viking houses looked like this.
The houses were covered with grass and earth.
This kept the people warm
in the cold winter.

15

distaff

spindle

This is the living room of the house.
One woman is cooking a meal.
She cooks over a big fire.
The smoke goes through a hole in the roof.
16

weaving loom

Everybody is helping to make clothes.
The boy is spinning thread.
One woman is weaving cloth.
Another is sewing a dress.

a Viking warrior

helmet —

shield

chain
mail
armour

For farming Vikings wore clothes like this.
But for fighting
they had helmets and weapons.

18

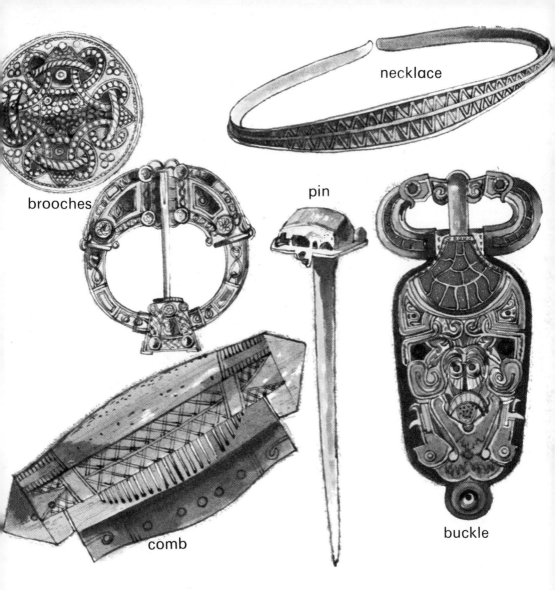

brooches

necklace

pin

comb

buckle

Here is some Viking jewellery.
Vikings often used brooches
to fasten their clothes.
They used pins and buckles too.

stirrup

spur

collar

Vikings often rode on horses.
Sometimes they used horses to pull carts.
Then the horse wore a collar.

20

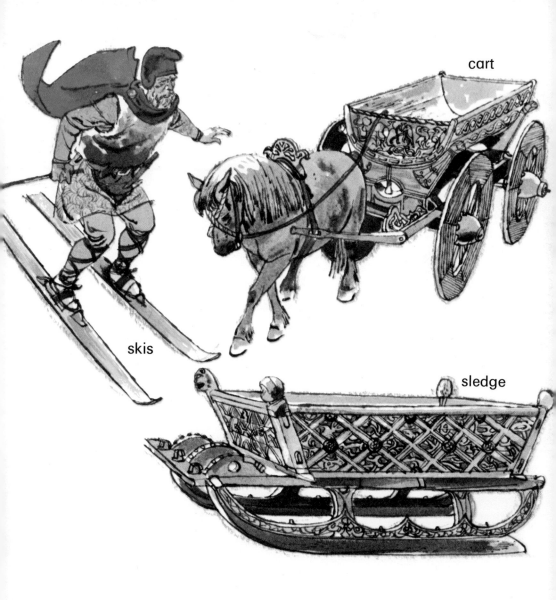

cart

skis

sledge

Vikings used sledges in the winter.
The carts could not move in deep snow.
Vikings were the first people to use skis.

21

In the winter Viking chiefs had feasts.
Everybody came.
Sometimes Viking feasts lasted all night.

tapestry

There is a storyteller at this feast.
He is telling a story
from the tapestry on the wall.
Tapestries are cloth pictures.

Odin

Thor

Viking stories are called sagas.
Sagas were often about Viking gods.
Odin rode on a horse with eight legs.
Thor fought with a dragon.

Vikings hiding
the grave

tent

longship hidden
under the earth

When important Vikings died
they were buried in ships.
Their treasure was put in with them.
People have found Viking ships
under the ground.

See if you can make
your own Viking longship, like this.
You can make one out of card.

Cut out two shapes like the top picture.
Fasten the shapes to boxes.
Decorate it yourself.

Index